DAY TRADING FOR BEGINNERS 2020

A guide for learn in one day risk management, discipline and trading psychology, strategy, invest, money, gold, Bitcoin, cryptocurrency, Nasdaq, petroleum, option

LUCKY STAFFORD

CHAPTER ONE	3
Day Trading: An Introduction	3
CHAPTER TWO	14
Day Trading Instruments	14
CHAPTER THREE	44
Trading Platforms, Tools, Brokers	44
CHAPTER FOUR	81
Risk & Money Management	81
CHAPTER FIVE	102
Day Trading Psychology	102

CHAPTER ONE

Day Trading: An Introduction

There was a time when the only individuals that could trade actively in the stock exchange were people working for big financial institutions, brokerages, and trading houses. However, with the development of the web and internet trading homes, agents have made it a lot easier for the typical individual investor to invest in on the sport.

Day trading can prove to be an extremely rewarding career, provided that you do it correctly. However, in addition, it can be somewhat hard for novices--particularly for people that aren't totally prepared with a strategy. The most experienced day dealers may reach rough patches and expertise losses. Therefore, just what is day trading and how can this function?

KEY TAKEAWAYS

- Day dealers are busy traders who implement intraday plans to gain off cost changes for any particular asset.
- Day trading uses a huge array of strategies and techniques to capitalize on perceived market inefficiencies.

- Day trading is frequently characterized by specialized evaluation and takes a high amount of self-discipline and objectivity.

The Fundamentals of Day Trading

Day Trading is described as the sale and purchase of a security within one trading day. It may happen in almost any market but is most frequent in the foreign exchange (forex) and stock markets) Day traders are generally well-educated and well-funded. They utilize high levels of leverage and short-term trading strategies to capitalize on small price movements in highly liquid stocks or currencies.

Day Traders are attuned to events which cause short-term market movements. Trading the information is a favorite technique. Scheduled announcements like economic statistics, company earnings or interest rates are subject to market expectations and marketplace psychology. Markets respond when those expectations aren't fulfilled or are surpassed, usually with abrupt, significant movements, which may reap traders.

Day Traders utilize numerous intraday strategies. These plans include:

- Scalping, that tries to create numerous tiny gains on little prices changes during the afternoon
- Range trading, which mostly utilizes resistance and support levels to ascertain their purchase and sell decisions
- News-based trading, which generally seizes trading opportunities out of the increased volatility about information events
- High-frequency trading (HFT) approaches using sophisticated calculations to exploit short-term or small market inefficiencies

A Controversial Practice

The Profit possibility of day trading is maybe among the most debated and misunderstood issues on Wall Street. Internet day trading scams have enticed amateurs by promising huge returns in a brief period. The thought that this sort of trading is that a hedging strategy persists. Some individual's day trade without adequate understanding. However there are traders that make a prosperous living even though --or maybe because of the dangers.

Many Professional money managers and financial advisors shy away from day trading claiming that, generally, the payoff doesn't warrant the risk. Conversely, those who do evening commerce insist there's gain to be made. Day trading profitably is potential, however, the success rate is essentially reduced due to the sophistication and mandatory risk of day trading in combination with the associated scams. Additionally, economists and financial professionals alike assert that long intervals, active trading plans often underperform a more fundamental passive indicator plan, particularly after taxes and fees are taken into consideration.

Day Trading isn't appropriate for everybody and entails significant risks. What's more, it requires a thorough comprehension of how the markets operate and various strategies for profiting in the brief term. While we recall the success stories of individuals who struck it rich as a day trader, keep in mind that many don't many will fizzle out and most will only barely stay afloat. What's more, do not underestimate the role that luck and decent time playwhile ability is surely a component, a rout of terrible fortune can sink even the most experienced day trader.

Attributes Of a Day Trader

Professional Day dealers --those who exchange for a living as opposed to as a hobby--are usually well-established within the specialty. They generally have in-depth understanding of the market, also. Here are a Few of the requirements required for a successful day trader:

Knowledge and expertise from the market

Folks who try to day trade with no understanding of market fundamentals frequently eliminate money. Technical analysis and graph reading is a fantastic ability for a day trader to get, but with no broader comprehension of the market you are in and the resources which exist in that current market, graphs might be deceiving. Do your due diligence and also comprehend the specific the inner workings of the merchandise that you trade.

Sufficient Funding

Day Traders use just threat capital that they may afford to lose. Does this protect them from financial ruin, but additionally, it can help remove emotion out of their trading. A great deal of funds is frequently vital to capitalize effectively on intraday price moves. Having access to your margin accounts can be crucial, because volatile swings may incur margin calls on short notice.

Plan

A Dealer requires an edge over the rest of the marketplace. There are many unique strategies day traders utilize such as swing trading, arbitrage, and trading information. These plans are refined until they produce consistent profits and effectively limit losses.

Discipline

A Profitable approach is useless without subject. Many day traders wind up losing a great deal of cash because they don't make transactions that meet their particular standards. As they state, "Plan the commerce and trade the strategy." Success is impossible without subject.

To Gain, day traders rely heavily on volatility on the marketplace. A stock could be appealing to your day trader when it moves a good deal throughout the day. That could occur due to a range of different things such as a sales report, investor sentiment, or perhaps overall economic or business news.

Day Traders also prefer stocks which are heavily liquid since that gives them the opportunity to modify their position without changing the purchase price of this inventory. When a stock price goes higher, traders might take a buy position. If the price goes, a dealer may opt to short-sell so that he can gain when it drops.

Regardless Of what approach a day dealer uses, they are usually seeking to exchange a stock that moves... a whole lot.

Day Trading for a Living

There are two key divisions of professional day traders: individuals who operate independently or those who work to get a bigger institution. Most day traders who trade for a living work for a big institution. These dealers have an edge since they have access to a guide line, a trading desk, considerable quantities of leverage and capital, expensive analytical applications, plus even more. These dealers are generally searching for easy profits which may be drawn up out of arbitrage opportunities and information events, and such tools permit them to capitalize on those less risky day transactions prior to individual traders may respond.

Individual Traders frequently handle other people's money or just trade with their very own. Few of these have access to a trading desk, however they frequently have strong ties into some broker (because of the large sums they invest on commissions) and access to additional sources. On the other hand, the limited extent of those funds prevents them from competing directly with daily dealers. Rather, they have to take more risks. Individual traders normally commerce using technical evaluation and swing transactions --coupled with a leverage--to make sufficient profits on these little price movements in highly liquid stocks.

Day Trading demands accessibility to a number of the very complicated financial services and tools in the market. Day traders typically demand:

Access Into a trading desk

This is usually reserved for dealers working for bigger institutions or people who handle considerable quantities of money. The working desk provides these dealers with immediate purchase executions, which can be especially important when sharp price movements happen. By way of instance, when an acquisition is announced, day traders considering merger arbitrage may place their orders until the remainder of the marketplace can benefit from the cost differential.

Multiple News resources

News Provides the vast majority of chances from that day traders vie, therefore it's critical to be the first to know when something important occurs. The normal trading area includes entry to the Dow Jones Newswire, continuous coverage of CNBC and other news organizations, and applications that continuously analyzes news resources for stories that are important.

Analytical Applications

Trading Applications is a costly requirement for many day traders. People who rely on specialized signs or swing transactions rely more on applications than information. This computer software might be distinguished by the following:

- Automated pattern recognition: This usually means the trading system identifies technical indicators such as flags and stations, or much more complicated indicators like Elliott Wave patterns.
- Genetic and neural software: These are applications using neural networks and genetic algorithms to ideal trading systems to create more precise predictions of future price moves.

- Broker integration: a few of those applications even interface directly with all the broker that allows for a quick and also automatic execution of transactions. This helps for eliminating emotion out of trading and enhancing execution times.
- Backtesting: This enables traders to check out how a particular strategy could have performed before so as to predict more precisely how it will function in the long run. Remember that past performance isn't necessarily indicative of future results.

Combined, those tools provide traders having an edge over the rest of the market. It's simple to see why, with them, so many inexperienced traders eliminate money.

If You Start Day Trading?

As Mentioned previously, day trading for a profession can be quite hard and a significant struggle. To begin with, you have to come in having some understanding of the trading world and also have a fantastic idea of your risk tolerance, funds, and intentions.

Day trading can be a profession which needs a whole lot of time. If you would like to perfect your plans --once you have mastered, naturally --and also earn money, you are going to need to devote a great deal of time for this. This is not something that you can do part-time or should you have the urge. You've got to be completely invested in it.

Should you decide that the delight of trading is ideal for you, don't forget to start little. Focus on some stocks instead of entering the industry head-first and sporting yourself lean. Going out will just complicate your trading plan and also can mean huge losses.

Eventually, remain cool and attempt to keep the emotion from your transactions. The more you are able to accomplish that, the further you will have the ability to stick with your strategy. Maintaining a level head lets you keep your attention when keeping you on the road you have chosen to return.
If you observe these basic guidelines, you can be led for a fantastic career in trading.

The Bottom Line

Even though Day trading has become a bit of a contentious occurrence, it can be a viable means to bring in profit. Day dealers, both individual and institutional, play a significant role in the market by maintaining the markets liquid and efficient. While popular amongst inexperienced dealers, it ought to be left mostly to people with the resources and skills required to be successful.

CHAPTER TWO

Day Trading Instruments

STOCK

An inventory (also Called equity) is a Safety that represents the possession of a portion of a company. This frees the owner of the inventory to some percentage of their company's assets and gains equivalent to just how much stock they have. Components of inventory are called "stocks".

Stocks are bought and sold mostly on stock trades, even though there may be personal sales too, and will be the basis of several different investors' portfolios. These trades must conform to government regulations that are supposed to protect investors from fraudulent practices. Historically, they've outperformed many other investments within the long term. These investments can be bought from many online stock brokers. Stock investment differs considerably from property investment.

KEY TAKEAWAYS
- A stock is a sort of security that suggests that the holder has proportionate ownership in the issuing company.
- Businesses difficulty (sell) stock to increase funds to run their companies. There are two chief types of stock: common and preferred.
- Stocks are purchased and sold mostly on stock trades, even though there may be personal sales too, and they're the basis of just about any portfolio.
- Historically, they've outperformed many other investments over the long term.

Recognizing Stocks

Corporations issue (sell) stock to increase money to operate their Companies. The holder of inventory (a shareholder) has bought a bit of the company and, based on the sort of stocks held, might have a claim to part of its earnings and assets. To put it differently, a shareholder is currently an owner of the issuing firm. Ownership is determined by the amount of shares a individual possesses relative to the amount of outstanding shares. As an instance, if a business has 1,000 shares of stock outstanding and a single individual owns 100 shares, then that individual would own and possess claim to 10 percent of the organization's earnings and assets.

Stock holders don't have businesses; they have stocks issued by companies. But businesses are a distinctive kind of business because the law treats them as authorized persons. To put it differently, corporations file taxation, can borrow, can own land, may be sued, etc. The thought that a company is a "person" means that the company possesses its assets. A corporate office filled with seats and tables belongs to the company, also not into the shareholders.

This differentiation is significant because corporate land is lawfully separated in the land of shareholders, which restricts the liability of the company and the shareholder. In case the company goes bankrupt, a judge can order all its assets offered -- however your personal assets aren't in danger. The court can't even make you sell your stocks, even though the value of your stocks will have dropped drastically. Likewise, if a significant shareholder goes bankrupt, she can't sell the organization's assets to pay her off creditors.

Stockholders and Fiscal Ownership
What shareholders really have are stocks issued by the company; And the company owns the resources held by a company. Therefore, in the event that you have 33 percent of the stocks of a business, it's erroneous to argue that you have one third of the firm; it's rather right to say that you have 100 percent of one third of their firm's shares. Shareholders can't

do as they please using a company or its resources. A shareholder cannot walk outside with a seat because the company possesses that seat, not the shareholder. This is referred to as the "separation of possession and management"

Owning stock provides you the right to vote in person meetings, receive dividends (which would be the firm's gains) if and when they're dispersed, and it provides you the right to sell your stocks to someone else.

If You Have a Vast Majority of stocks, your voting power increases so you're able to indirectly control the management of a business by devoting its board of supervisors. This becomes apparent when one business buys the following: that the acquiring company does not go about buying up the construction, the seats, the workers; it buys all of the stocks. The board of supervisors is accountable for raising the worth of the company, and frequently does this by hiring professional managers, or officials, like the Chief Executive Officer, or even CEO.

For many average shareholders, not being able to manage the Firm Is not such a huge thing. The significance of being a customer is that you're eligible for a part of the organization's gains, and that, as we'll see, is the basis of a stock's worth.

The more stocks you have, the bigger the section of the earnings you get. Many stocks, but do not cover out dividends, and rather reinvest profits back to developing the firm. All these retained earnings, nevertheless, are still represented in the worth of a stock exchange.

Common vs. Preferred Stock
There are two chief types of inventory: common and favored. Common inventory generally entitles the proprietor to vote at shareholders' meetings and to receive any dividends paid from the corporation. Preferred stockholders generally don't have voting rights, even though they have a greater claim on assets and earnings compared to common stockholders. By way of instance, owners of preferred stock (for instance, Larry Page) get dividends prior to common shareholders and have priority in case a firm goes bankrupt and is liquidated.

The very first typical stock ever issued was from the Dutch East India Company in 1602.

Companies can issue new stocks whenever there's a need to increase Additional money. This procedure dilutes the possession and rights of existing shareholders (as long as they don't purchase any of their newest offerings). Businesses may also take part in stock buy-backs that would benefit present investors as it might cause their stocks to appreciate in value.

Stocks Bonds

Stocks have been issued by companies to raise funds, paid-up or discuss, in Order to grow the company or undertake new jobs. There are significant distinctions between if someone buys stocks directly from the business once it issues them (from the main market) or by the other shareholder (about the secondary marketplace). After the company issues shares, it does so in exchange for cash.

Bonds are basically distinct from shares in many of ways. To begin with, bondholders are lenders to the company, and therefore are eligible for interest in addition to payment of principal. Creditors have legal priority along with other stakeholders in case of a bankruptcy and will be made first if a business is forced to sell assets so as to repay them. Shareholders, on the other hand, are in line and frequently receive nothing, or only pennies on the dollar, in case of bankruptcy. This suggests that stocks are inherently riskier investments which bonds.

FUTURES

Futures are derivative financial contracts which obligate the parties to transact an advantage at a predetermined future date and cost. Here, the purchaser must buy or the vendor have to sell the underlying asset in the established price, irrespective of the current market price in the expiry date.

Underlying assets consist of physical commodities or other monetary tools. Futures contracts detail the amount of the underlying asset and therefore are standardized to facilitate trading on a futures. Futures May be used for hedging or commerce speculation.

KEY TAKEAWAYS

- Inventories are monetary contracts obligating the buyer to buy an advantage or the vendor to sell an advantage and also have a predetermined future date and cost.
- A futures contract enables an investor to speculate on the management of a security, commodity, or a monetary tool.
- Futures are utilized to hedge the price movement of the underlying asset to help avoid losses from adverse price fluctuations.

Futures Described

Futures--too known as futures contracts--enable traders to lock in a cost of their underlying asset or product. These contracts have expirations dates and establish costs which are well known up front. Futures are recognized by their expiry month. By way of instance, a December gold futures contract expires in December. The expression stocks often signify the general sector. But, There Are Lots of Kinds of futures contracts available for trading such as:

- Commodities futures like in crude petroleum, natural gas, corn, and wheat
- Stock index futures like the S&P 500 Index
- Money stocks such as those for the euro and the British pound
- Precious metal futures for silver and gold
- U.S. Treasury futures for bonds and other commodities

It is Important to be aware the differentiation between futures and options. Alternatives contracts give the holder the right to purchase or sell the underlying advantage in the beginning, whereas the holder of a futures contract is obligated to meet the conditions of the contract.

Advantages

· Investors may use futures contracts to speculate on the path in the Purchase Price of an underlying advantage

· Companies can hedge the Cost of the raw materials or merchandise they market to protect against adverse price moves

· Futures contracts may only require a deposit of some fraction of the contract number with a broker

Disadvantages

· Investors have a danger they can lose more than the initial margin amount since futures leverage

· Purchasing a futures contract may cause a Business that hedged to overlook positive price moves

· Margin May be double-edged sword significance profits are amplified but are reductions

Using Futures

The Futures markets typically utilize high leverage. Leverage means the dealer doesn't have to put up 100 percent of their contracts worth amount when entering a transaction. Rather, the agent would need an initial margin sum, which is made up of small percent of the entire contract value. The total held by the agent may fluctuate based upon how big their contract, the creditworthiness of the investor, as well as the agent's terms and conditions.

The Exchange at which the future transactions will ascertain whether the contract is for physical shipping or whether it could be cash settled. A company can enter into a tangible shipping contract to lock --hedge--the cost of a commodity they want for manufacturing. But most futures contracts are out of dealers that speculate on the transaction. These contracts are closed out or netted--that the gap in the initial trade and final transaction price--and therefore are money settled.

Futures Speculation
A Futures contract enables a dealer to speculate on the path of motion of a commodity's price.

If a Trader purchased a futures contract and the cost of the commodity climbed and was trading over the initial contract price at expiration, then they'd have a gain. Prior to expiration, the purchase trade--extended standing --could be unwound with a market exchange for exactly the exact same amount in the present cost effectively shutting the extended standing.

The gap between the costs of both contracts will be money settled at the investor's brokerage accounts, and no actual product will change hands. On the other hand, the dealer may also lose if the product's price was lower than the cost specified in the futures contract.

Speculators May also take a brief or market speculative position should they forecast the cost of the underlying asset will collapse. In the event the cost does decrease, the dealer will require an offsetting position to shut the contract. The net difference could be settled in the expiration of this contract. An investor could realize a profit if the underlying asset's cost was under the contract price and a reduction in the event the present cost was over the contract price.

It is Important to be aware that trading margin allows for a much larger place compared to the total held by the broker account. Because of this, margin investing could amplify profits, but it can also magnify losses. Envision a dealer with a $5,000 agent accounts balance and can be in a trade to get a $50,000 place in crude oil. If the amount of oil proceed contrary to their commerce, they could incur losses which far surpass the account's $5,000 initial allowance amount. In cases like this, the agent would earn a margin call requiring extra funds be deposited to pay the market declines.

Futures Hedging

Futures May be utilized to hedge the cost movement of the underlying asset. Here, the target is to avoid losses from possibly adverse price fluctuations rather than to speculate. Lots of businesses which input hedges are using--or oftentimes generating --that the underlying asset.

For Example, a corn farmer may use futures to lock in a particular cost for selling their corn harvest. By doing this they reduce their risk and ensure they'll obtain the fixed cost. If the purchase price of corn diminished, the corporation would have a profit on the market to offset losses from selling the corn in the market. With this kind of a profit and loss offsetting each other, the payoff effectively locks at a decent market price.

How Do Futures Deal Work?

Legislation of Futures

The futures markets have been controlled by the Commodity Futures Trading Commission (CFTC). The CFTC is a national agency created by Congress in 1974 to guarantee the integrity of futures pricing, such as preventing abusive trading practices, fraud, and regulating broker companies engaged in futures trading.

Selecting a Futures Broker

Purchasing stocks or any other financial tools needs a broker. Stock brokers offer access to the markets and exchanges in which these investments are transacted. The practice of picking a broker and locating investments that match your requirements can be a bewildering procedure.

Actual World Example of Futures

Let us say a trader needs to Speculate on the purchase price of crude oil by entering into a futures contract in May with the anticipation that the cost will be greater by years-end. The December crude oil futures contract is trading at $50 and the dealer locks from the contract.

Since oil is traded in increments of 1,000 barrels, the investor currently has a place worth $50,000 of crude petroleum (1,000 x $50 = $50,000). On the other hand, the dealer is only going to must pay a portion of the sum up front--the first margin they follow along with the agent.

From May to December, the Purchase Price of Oil changes as will the value of the futures contract. If oil's cost becomes too explosive, the agent may request additional funds to be deposited to the margin accounts --a maintenance allowance.

In December, the end date of the contract is coming, which will be on the third Friday of this month. The cost of crude oil has climbed to $65, and the dealer sells the contract to leave the position. The internet distinction is cash settled, and they make $15,000, less any commissions and fees from the agent ($65 - $50 = $15 x 1000 = $15,000).

But if the cost oil had dropped to $40 rather, the investor could have lost $10,000 ($40 - $50 = negative $10 x 1000 = negative $10,000.

GETTING ACQUAINTED WITH OPTIONS TRADING

Trading options is quite distinct from trading stocks since choices have different attributes from stocks. It is important for traders to choose some opportunity to comprehend the terminology and theories involved in choices before investing in them.

Alternatives are financial derivatives, which means they derive their value from the underlying security or inventory. Options give the purchaser the right, but not the obligation, to purchase or sell the underlying stock in a pre-determined cost.

KEY TAKEAWAYS
- Alternatives give a buyer the right, but not the obligation, to buy (call) or sell (put) the underlying stock in a pre-determined cost known as the strike price.
- Alternatives have a price associated with them, called a premium, and an expiry date.
- A call option is rewarding once the strike price is below the stock's market price because the dealer can purchase the stock at a lower cost.
- A put option is rewarding once the attack is greater than the stock's market price because the dealer may sell the inventory at a greater cost.

Choices 101

Trading stocks could be compared to Gambling at a casino: You are betting against the house, so if most of the clients have an unbelievable series of luck, they can all win.

Trading choices is similar to gambling on horses at the racetrack: Every person bets against the rest of the individuals there. The track simply requires a little cut for supplying the facilities. So trading choices, such as betting at the horse trail, is a zero-sum game. The alternative buyer's profit is your alternative seller's reduction and vice versa.

1 significant difference between shares and options will be that stocks give you a little bit of ownership in a business, while alternatives are only contracts that provide you the best to purchase or sell the stock at a particular price by a particular date.

It is important to keep in mind there are two sides for each choice trade: a purchaser and a vendor. To put it differently, for every option purchased, there is always somebody else promoting it.

Kinds of Choices

The 2 kinds of choices are puts and calls. When you Purchase a call alternative, you've got the right, but not the obligation, to buy a stock at a set cost, known as the strike cost, any time before the option expires. When you purchase a set option, you've got the right, but not the obligation, to sell a stock at the strike price any time prior to the expiry date.

When folks sell alternatives, they effectively produce a safety that did not exist earlier. This is referred to as composing a choice, and it clarifies one of the chief resources of alternatives since neither the affiliated company nor the choices exchange problems that the choices.

When you compose a call, You Might Be obligated to sell stocks at the Strike price any time prior to the expiry date. If you write a place, you might be bound to purchase stocks at the strike price any time prior to expiry.

Additionally, there are two primary trends of choices: European and American. An American-style Alternative May be exercised at any time between the date of order and the expiry date. A European-style alternative can only be exercised on the expiry date. Most exchange traded options are American style, and all stock options are American style. Many index options are European design.

Option Pricing

The purchase price of an option is known as the premium. The purchaser of an Option can not lose over the original premium paid for the contract, regardless of what occurs to the inherent security. Hence that the risk to the purchaser is not greater than the total paid for the option. The profit possible, on the other hand, is unlimited.

In exchange for the premium received by the buyer, the vendor of an Option assumes the possibility of needing to send (in case a call option) or accepting delivery (when a put option) of the shares of this inventory. Unless that alternative is insured by a different alternative or some position in the underlying stock, the vendor's reduction could be open-ended, meaning that the vendor can lose a whole lot more than the initial premium obtained.

Please be aware that options aren't available at any price. Stock Choices are usually traded with strike prices in periods of $0.50 or $1, but could also be in periods of $2.50 and $5 to get higher-priced stocks. Additionally, only hit costs within a reasonable range around the current stock price are usually traded. Far in- or out-of-the-money options may not be accessible.

Choice Profitability

After the strike price of a call option is over the current cost of the inventory, the telephone isn't rewarding or out-of-the-money. To put it differently, an investor isn't going to purchase a stock at a higher price (the attack) compared to the current market price of this inventory. After the call option strike price is below the stock's cost, it is considered in-the-money because the investor can purchase the stock for a lesser cost than at the present sector.

Set options will be the specific opposite. They are considered Out-of-the-money once the strike price is below the stock price because an investor would not sell the inventory at a lower price (the attack) than at the marketplace. Set options are in-the-money once the strike price is above the stock price since investors may sell the inventory in the greater (strike) price than the market cost of this inventory.

Expiration Dates

All inventory options expire on a particular date, known as the expiration date. For Normal listed choices, this may be up to eight months from the date that the options are listed for trading. Longer-term alternative contracts, known as long term equity anticipation securities (LEAPS), will also be available on a lot of stocks. All these may have expiration dates up to three years in the record date.

Options expire at market close on Friday, unless it falls onto a Market vacation, in which event expiration is transferred back 1 business day. Monthly options expire on the third Friday of the expiry month, while each week options expire on every one of the other Fridays per month.

Unlike stocks of inventory, that are in a three-day settlement interval, Options settle the following day. To be able to settle the expiry date, you need to work out or exchange the choice at the close of the afternoon on Friday.

FOREX -- FX

Forex (FX) is the market where various national monies are exchanged. The foreign exchange market is the biggest, most liquid marketplace on the planet, using trillions of bucks changing hands daily. There's not any centralized place, instead the currency marketplace is an electronic network of banks, agents, associations, and individual dealers (mainly trading through banks or brokers).

Many entities, from financial institutions to individual traders, have money wants, and might also speculate on the management of a specific set of monies motion. They post their own orders to purchase and sell currencies on the community so that they could socialize with other money orders from different parties.

The foreign exchange market is open 24 hours each day, five days per week, except for vacations. Currencies may still exchange on a vacation if the country/global marketplace is open for business.

KEY TAKEAWAYS
- The currency market is a community of associations, allowing for trading 24 hours a day, five times each

week, with the exception of if all markets have been closed due to a holiday.
- Retail traders may start a forex account then buy and sell currencies. A gain or loss results in the difference in cost the money pair was purchased and sold in the slightest.
- Forwards and futures are just another means to take part in the foreign exchange industry. Forwards are customizable using the monies exchanged following expiry. Futures aren't customizable and are more easily used by speculators, however, the rankings are usually closed prior to expiry (to prevent settlement).
- The currency market is the biggest financial market on earth.

Retail traders don't wish to deliver the whole quantity of money they're trading. Rather, they wish to profit on cost differences in currencies with time. As a result of this, agent's rollover positions every day.

Forex Market Basics

Forex Pairs and Quotes

When trading monies, they're recorded in pairs, for example as USD/CAD, EUR/USD, or USD/JPY. These signify the U.S. dollar (USD) versus the Canadian dollar (CAD), the Euro

(EUR) versus the USD and the USD versus the Japanese Yen (JPY).

There'll also be a cost related to every group, for example 1.2569. Whether this cost was connected with the USD/CAD set it usually means it prices 1.2569 CAD to purchase one USD. If the purchase price rises to 1.3336, afterward it currently costs 1.3336 CAD to purchase one USD. The USD has increased in value (CAD reduction) since it currently costs more CAD to purchase one USD.

Forex Lots

In the currency market currencies exchange in a lot, known as micro, miniature, and regular lots. A micro great deal is 1000 value of a specific currency, a miniature bunch is 10,000, and also a normal lot is 100,000. That can be different than when you visit a lender and need $450 traded for your journey. When investing in the digital foreign exchange market, transactions happen in set cubes of money, but you can exchange as many cubes as you'd like. As an instance, you can exchange seven micro tons (7,000) or 3 miniature lots (30,000) or even 75 standard lots (750,000), for instance)

How Big Is the Forex?

The Foreign Exchange Market is exceptional for many reasons, largely due to its size. Trading quantity is usually very large. For example, trading in foreign exchange markets totaled $5.1 trillion daily at April 2016, according to the Bank for International Settlements.

The biggest international exchange markets are located in important global financial centers such as London, New York, Singapore, Tokyo, Frankfurt, Hong Kong, and Sydney.

How to Trade from the Forex

The forex marketplace is available 24 hours each day, five days each week across important financial centres throughout the world. This usually means you could purchase or sell currencies in any given time throughout the week.

From a historic perspective, foreign exchange trading has been largely restricted to governments, big businesses, and hedge funds. However, in the present world, trading currencies is as simple as a click of mouse. Access is no problem, so anybody can get it done. Many investment Companies, banks, and retail currency brokers give the opportunity for people to start Accounts and also to exchange currencies.

When investing in the Foreign Exchange Market, You are purchasing or selling the currency of a specific country, relative to some other currency. But there is no actual exchange of cash from 1 party to another. That is what happens in a Currency kiosk--consider a tourist visiting Times Square in Nyc from Japan. He can be turning his bodily yen to real U.S. dollar money (and might be billed a commission to do this) so that he could spend his money while he is traveling. But in the sphere of digital markets, dealers are often able in a particular currency, together with the expectation that there'll be some upward motion and strength in the money they are purchasing (or weakness whenever they are selling) so that they can earn a profit.

A money is obviously traded relative to some other currency. Should you market a money, you're purchasing a different, and if you purchase a money you're selling another. From the digital trading globe, a gain is made about the gap between your trade rates.

Spot Transactions

A place market bargain is for instant shipping, which can be described as two business days for most currency pairs. The significant exception is that the sale or purchase of USD/CAD, which can be settled in 1 business day. The company day calculation excludes Saturdays, Sundays, and legal holidays in currency of the traded group. Throughout the Christmas and Easter season, some place trades may take as long as six times to repay. Funds are traded on the settlement date, maybe not the trade date.

The U.S. buck is your most actively traded money. The euro is the most actively traded counter money, followed with the Japanese yen, British pound and Swiss franc.

Economy movements are driven by a combination of speculation, economic Strength and expansion, and interest rate differentials.

Forex (FX) Rollover

Retail traders do not typically need to take delivery of their monies they purchase. They're just interested in profiting on the gap between their trade rates. Due to this, most retail agents will mechanically "rollover" money positions in 5 p.m. EST daily.

The agent essentially resets the rankings and supplies either a charge or debit to the interest rate differential between the two currencies in the pairs being held. The transaction carries on and the dealer does not have to send or repay the trade. After the transaction is closed the dealer realizes their gain or loss based in their initial trade price and the cost they closed the transaction at. The rollover credits or debits may add to the advantage or detract from this.

Considering that the fx market is closed on Saturday and Sunday, the curiosity Rate debit or credit from such times is implemented on Wednesday. Thus, holding a position in 5 pm on Wednesday will end in being credited or debited triple the typical quantity.

Forex Forward Transactions

Any currency trade that settles to get a date later than place is Considered a "ahead." The cost is calculated by adjusting the spot rate to account for the gap in interest rates between the 2 currencies. The quantity of adjustment is known as "forward points" The forwards points represent just the interest rate differential between two niches. They aren't a prediction of how the place market will trade in a date later on. A forward is a tailor-made contract: it could be for almost any Sum of Money and can settle any date that is not a weekend or vacation. As in a place transaction, funds have been traded on the settlement date.

Forex (FX) Futures

A foreign exchange or money futures contract is an arrangement between two parties to provide a fixed quantity of money at a set date, also known as the expiry, later on. Futures contracts are traded on a market for place values of money and with place expiry dates. Contrary to a forward, the conditions of a futures contract are non-negotiable. A gain is made on the gap between the costs the contract has been purchased and sold in. Many speculators do not hold futures contracts before expiration, as that will demand they deliver/settle the money the contract signifies. Rather, speculators purchase and market the contracts before expiration, realizing their gains or losses in their trades.

Forex Market stinks

There are some significant differences between the currency and other markets.

Fewer Rules

This means investors are not held to as stringent criteria or Regulations as the ones from the stock, futures or alternatives markets. There aren't any clearing homes and no fundamental bodies which manage the whole foreign exchange marketplace. It is possible to short-sell at any moment since in forex you are not ever really shorting; should you sell one currency you're purchasing another.

Prices and Commissions

Considering that the market is unregulated, how agents charge commissions and Commissions will be different. Most forex brokers earn money by signing up the disperse on money pairs. Other people generate income by charging a commission, which varies depending on the total amount of money traded. Some agents use these two approaches.

Total Access

There is no cut-off regarding if you can and can't trade. Since the Marketplace is available 24 hours every day, it is possible to exchange at any given time of the day. The exclusion is weekends, or whenever no international financial centre is available because of a vacation.

Leverage

The currency market permits for leverage around 50:1 At the U.S. and much higher in certain areas of the planet. That usually means a dealer can start an account for $1,000 and purchase or sell up to $50,000 in money, for instance. Leverage is a sword that is mythical; it magnifies both gains and losses.

Instance of Forex Transactions

Assume a dealer thinks that the EUR will appreciate against the USD. Another way of considering this is that the USD will fall relative to the EUR.

They purchase the EUR/USD in 1.2500 and buy $5,000 worth of money. Later that afternoon the cost has risen to 1.2550. The dealer is up $25 (5000 * 0.0050). If the cost dropped to 1.2430, the dealer would be dropping $35 (5000 * 0.0070).

Money prices are constantly moving, so the trader can choose to hold the position immediately. The agent will rollover the standing, causing a debit or credit depending on the interest rate differential between the Eurozone and the U.S. In the event the Eurozone has a rate of interest of 4 percent and the U.S. has a rate of interest of 3 percent, the dealer possesses the greater interest rate money since they purchased EUR. Accordingly, at rollover, the dealer should be given a little charge. When the EUR interest rate has been lower compared to USD speed then the dealer could be debited at rollover.

Rollover Can Impact a trading choice, particularly if the transaction could be held for the long run. Massive gaps in interest rates may lead to significant credits or debits every day, which could considerably improve or erode the gains (or raise or decrease losses) of this transaction.

Most agents also give leverage. Many agents in the U.S. offer Leverage around 50:1. Let us assume our dealer utilizes 10:1 leverage with this trade. If utilizing 10:1 leverage the dealer isn't needed to get $5,000 in their accounts, despite the fact that they are trading $5,000 value of money. They simply require $500. Provided that they have $500 and 10:1 leverage they could exchange $5,000 value of money. Should they use 20:1 leverage, then they simply need $250 within their accounts (since $250 * 20 = $5,000).

Making a gain of $25 very quickly thinking about the trader only wants $500 or $250 from the funds (or less if using more leverage), reveals the power of leverage. The flip side is that when this dealer just had $250 in their accounts and the transaction went against them they might lose their funds fast.

Its recommended traders handle their place size and Control their risk in order that no single transaction ends in a sizable reduction.

CHAPTER THREE

Trading Platforms, Tools, Brokers

What's a Trading Platform?

A trading platform is software used for trading: opening, closing, and managing market positions through a fiscal intermediary such as an internet broker. Online trading programs are often provided by agents either at no cost or at a discount fee in exchange for keeping a funded account or making a predetermined variety of transactions each month. The finest trading platforms provide a mixture of powerful features and reduced prices.

KEY TAKEAWAYS

- Trading programs are software tools used to handle and implement market rankings.
- Platforms vary from fundamental order entry displays for novice investors to complicated and complex toolkits with live streaming quotes and charts for advanced traders.

Traders and traders must take numerous factors into account and equilibrium trade-offs when choosing a trading platform.

Principles of Trading Platform

A trading platform is the application That Permits traders and investors to place transactions and track accounts through fiscal intermediaries. Oftentimes, trading programs will come bundled together with different characteristics, such as real time quotations, charting programs, news feeds, as well as superior research. Platforms might also be especially tailored to certain markets, like stocks, monies, alternatives, or futures markets.

There are two different types of trading platforms: prop platforms and industrial platforms. As their title suggests, commercial systems have been aimed at day traders and retail investors. They're characterized by ease-of-use along with also a range of useful features, such as news feeds and graphs, for investor education and study. Prop platforms, on the other hand, are customized platforms developed with big brokerages to match their particular needs and trading style.

Dealers use an assortment of different trading platforms based on their trading design and quantity.

Selecting a Platform

When picking between trading platforms, both investors and traders should consider both the charges involved and attributes available. Day dealers along with other short-term traders might need attributes like Grade two quotations and market manufacturer depth charts to help out with decision-making, whilst choices traders might need tools which are particularly designed to picture options plans.

Fees are another significant consideration when picking trading platforms. By way of instance, traders that use scalping for a trading approach may gravitate towards platforms using reduced prices. Generally, lower prices are almost always preferable but there might be trade-offs to take into account. By way of instance, low prices might not be valuable if they interpret to fewer attributes and informational study.

Some trading platforms can be reverted to a Particular intermediary or even Agent, though other trading platforms are only accessible when working with a specific broker or agent. Because of this, investors should also consider the standing of the intermediary or agent before committing to a certain trading platform to implement trades and handle their account.

Ultimately, trading platforms might have particular requirements to be eligible Due to their usage. By way of instance, day trading platforms might require that dealers have $25,000 at equity inside their account and be qualified for margin trading, whereas alternatives platforms might require approval to exchange a variety of kinds of choices prior to having the ability to utilize the trading platform.

Popular Trading Platforms

There are hundreds--or even thousands--of different trading platforms, including those four popular choices:

- Interactive Agents: Interactive Brokers is the most popular trading platform for professionals using reduced fees and accessibility to markets across the world.
- TradeStation: TradeStation is a favorite trading platform for algorithmic dealers who prefer to perform trading strategies utilizing automated scripts developed with Easy Language.
- TDAmeritrade: TDAmeritrade is a Favorite agent for both investors and traders, particularly after its acquisition of ThinkorSwim along with also the Maturation of this Trade Architect platforms.
- Robinhood: Robinhood is a commission-free trading platform aimed at millennial. It started off as a portable program and today has a web interface too. The platform makes cash from many sources, from interest on money in its account to promoting order flow to big brokerages.

- The very popular platform for all foreign exchange (forex) Marketplace participants is MetaTrader that will be a trading platform that interfaces with several distinct brokers. Its MQL scripting language is now a favorite tool for those seeking to automate trading in monies.

Selecting the Proper Day-Trading Software

Computer software have made it Simple to automate trading, particularly for short term intensive tasks like day trading, making the use of trading program popular. The discussion continues within the profit potential which will be realistically derived from day-trading actions utilizing online trading platforms, as broker fees and commissions are believed to eliminate the significant part of available gain possible. It thus becomes extremely important to choose the ideal day-trading software using a cost-benefit analysis, evaluation of its applicability to individual trading requirements and strategies, in addition to the features and functions you want.

Day trading is a currency trading action at which purchase or market positions are accepted and closed on precisely the exact same trading day with a goal to earn gains in smaller price differentials on large purchase volumes by regular buying and selling, typically on leverage.

KEY TAKEAWAYS
- Day trading applications demand tools and order entry systems that permit day traders to perform their job in an efficient and consistent method.
- These programs frequently feature automated trading based on parameters determined by the day dealer, allowing for orders to be routed to the marketplace faster than individual reflexes.
- Selecting the most appropriate day trading software program necessitates knowing the costs and advantages of every offering and in the event that you'll optimize its performance.

What's Day-Trading Software?

Day-trading software comprises a computer program, generally supplied by brokerage companies, to assist customers execute their day-trading actions in an efficient and timely way. They frequently automate analysis and input transactions in their own that allow traders to reap gains that would be tough to attain by mere mortals. By way of instance, a day dealer might find it impossible to manually monitor two technical indicators (such as 50- and 200-day moving averages) on three distinct shares of her or his choice, but an automatic day-trading software can certainly take action and put trades after the set standards are satisfied.

The characteristics and functions available can vary from 1 software package to another and can arrive in various versions. Aside from agents, independent sellers also give day-trading applications, which often have more advanced capabilities.

How Can Day-Trading Software Work?

Three fundamental characteristics of any day-trading software include:

- Functionality allowing the installment of trading system (based on technical indicators, news, trading signals or pattern recognition) from the trading platform
- Automated order-placing operate (generally with Immediate Market Access) after the standards are fulfilled
- Analytical instruments to keep assessment of Current holdings (if any), marketplace developments and attributes to accordingly behave on these

Any day-trading applications will demand a one-time installment of trading strategy together with establishing the trading limitations, setting the machine on live information and allowing it execute the transactions.

An example: Assume stock ABC is dual-listed on either the New York Stock Exchange (NYSE) and on Nasdaq. You're searching for arbitrage chances and there's a day-trading software available to this. You prepare the following:

Select inventory ABC for arbitrage and choose two markets (NYSE and Nasdaq) for trading.

Assuming both thighs of intraday exchange prices you a total of $0.10 per share for commission and brokerage; you plan to search for cost differentials between the two markets in excess of that sum. So that you place (state $0.20 or over) as the cost differential--i.e., the program must execute a simultaneous purchase and sell purchase just when the bidding and ask prices on the 2 markets are different by $0.20 (or much more).

Establish the amount of stocks to be purchased and sold in 1 sequence (say 10,000 stocks).

Permit this installment go live.

Say the Program explains that ABC has estimates of $62.10 on NYSE and $62.35 on Nasdaq (a differential of $0.25) for orders of over the established limit of 10,000 shares. The day-trading applications will commence trade as it fulfills with the specified standards, and will send orders into the two trades (purchase at reduced priced and market at even higher priced). If everything goes well, this day-trading applications will create ((62.35 -- 62.10) -- 0.10 = 0.15) * (10,000) = $1,500 of net gain for your dealer super-fast.

Further improvements in the aforementioned applications may include stop-loss attributes --state if just your purchase trade gets implemented but not the market. How should the day-trading applications proceed using the long standing? A few options can be contained as improved features in the program:

- Proceed to search for market chances at identified costs for a particular moment. If no opportunities are recognized in the designated period, square off the place at reduction.
- Set stop loss limits and square off the purchase order, if the limit is hit
- Change into an averaging strategy --purchase more shares at lower costs to Decrease the overall cost

Features and Functionality

The above is an example of arbitrage where gambling chances are short-lived. A Good Deal of these Kinds of day-trading actions can be installed via day-trading applications and so it's extremely important to pick the perfect one fitting your requirements. Some features of Great day-trading Applications:

- Platform freedom: Unless A dealer is operating exceptionally intricate calculations for Day-trading requiring high-end computers that are dedicated, it's sensible to go using an online program offering. Benefits include connectivity from anyplace, no manual installments of updates and no maintenance Prices. But If You're using highly sophisticated algorithms which need Sophisticated computing, then it's far better to consider committed computer-based Installable applications, even though that will be pricey.
- Your Particular needs daily trading: Are you currently observing a straightforward day-trading approach of moving-average monitoring on Stocks, or are you seeking to implement an intricate delta-neutral trading Strategy including stocks and options? Do you require a currency feed or are you currently trading on Specific products such as binary choices? Trusting the promises on stockbrokers' site content isn't enough to Know that the offering. Request a trial version also completely evaluate it during the first phase. Alternately, check the screen-by-screen Tutorial (if available) in the stockbroker or seller to clearly Know the ideal match for the day-trading needs.
- Added Attributes: Day trading efforts to capitalize on short-term price movements over the course of the

day. Such short term price movements are subsequently driven primarily by information and distribution and need (among other variables). Does your day-trading strategy demand information, graphs, Grade two info, exclusive connectivity into specific markets (such as OTC), special data feeds, etc.)? If so, are those contained in the applications or would the dealer need to subscribe to them individually from different resources, hence raising the price?

- Analytical Features: Pay attention to this record of analytical features it provides. Listed below are a couple of of these:
- Technical Indicators/Pattern Recognition: For dealers who try to gain from calling the upcoming cost level and management, a wealth of technical indicators can be obtained. When the dealer finalizes the specialized indicators to follow along, they ought to guarantee that the day-trading program affirms the essential automation for efficient processing of transactions based on the desirable technical index.
- Arbitrage Opportunities Recognition: To profit from the small cost difference of a dual-listed discuss on multiple niches, simultaneous buying (at a minimal cost market) and selling (at a high cost market) allows profit opportunities and can be among those typically followed approaches employing day-trading software.

This needs a link to both markets, the capacity to inspect cost differences as they happen and implement trades in a timely way.

- Mathematical model based approaches: Few automated trading approaches based on mathematical models exist--such as the delta-neutral trading system --which enable trading on a mixture of choices and its inherent security, where transactions are put to cancel negative and positive deltas so the portfolio delta is preserved at zero. The day-trading software ought to have the in-built intellect to estimate the recent holdings, confirm available market costs and implement trades for both equity and alternatives as required.
- Trend following approaches: Another massive collection of approaches commonly implemented via day-trading software.

Price and Other Factors

As can be seen in the above record, the sky is your limit with Computer programming and automatic software programs. Everything and anything can be automatic, with a great deal of customizations. Aside from choosing the ideal software, it's extremely important to check the identified approaches on historic data (ignoring the broker costs), evaluate the sensible gain potential and the effect of day-trading software expenses and just afterward go to get a subscription. That is just another area to assess, as many agents do provide backtesting performance in their applications platforms.

Price of applications: Is your software available as part of regular broker accounts or does this come in an extra price? Based upon your personal trading action, the cost-benefit analysis ought to be completed. Care needs to be taken to appraise the available variations and their attributes. Most trading software is sold free by default using a typical brokerage account but might not have all of the essential features fulfilling your trading requirements. Make certain to look at the expenses of greater versions which might be considerably greater than the conventional one. These prices should be disregarded in assessing the returns from trading and choices made based just on the realistic profits.

Cost Accuracy: Does the agent and day-trading software service NBBO (federal greatest bid and provide)? Agents that are NBBO participants are needed to execute the customer trades in the best available bid and ask price, making sure cost competitiveness. Determined by the country-specific regulations, agents may (or might not) be mandated to offer the very best bid and ask prices. Dealers trading global securities with global brokers and applications should think about confirming this to the particular sector.

Protective Characteristics: It is exciting to have applications make money for you personally, but security is paramount. With the improvement of technologies, there also exist "sniffing algorithms & applications" that try to spot the other-side orders on the industry. They're made to let their owners to gain out of it by "sensing" the orders on different hand. It'll be well worth considering if a day-trading applications is vulnerable to these sniffing or whether or not it has preventative characteristics to conceal vulnerability to other market participants.

The Main Point

You will find endless horizons to research with trading utilizing pc Applications and automatic software programs. It might be extremely exciting to earn money in the click of a button, however one wants to be completely conscious of what is going behind the scenes: Why Is the automatic order is becoming at the ideal price in the perfect market, can it be after the ideal strategy and so forth. A good deal of trading anomalies are credited to automated trading strategies. A comprehensive analysis of day-trading software using a transparent comprehension of your preferred trading strategy could allow individual traders to reap the advantages of automatic day trading.

The Complete Guide to Selecting an Online Stock Broker

Profitable investing requires you employ a broker service that contrasts with your investment objectives, educational needs and learning style. Particularly for new investors, picking out the best online stock broker that satisfies your requirements can mean the difference between a thrilling new revenue flow and irritating disappointment.

While there is no surefire approach to ensure investment yields, there's a way to put yourself up for success by simply choosing the online broker which most fits your requirements. Inside this guide, we will break everything down you ought to look for in your perfect broker , in the obvious (like whether or not the system permits you to exchange the securities you are considering) into the not-so-obvious (like just how simple it's to receive assistance from an authentic human once you require it).

KEY TAKEAWAYS
- Accessibility to the financial markets is simple and affordable because of many different discount brokers that run through internet platforms.
- Different online agents are optimized for a different sort of customer --from long term buy-and-hold novices to busy and sophisticated day dealers.

- Selecting the most appropriate online broker demands some due diligence to get the most for the money. Follow the steps and pointers in this guide to select appropriate.

Step 1: Know Your Requirements

Before You Begin clicking brokerage ads, Have a moment to hone in on what is most important for you in a trading platform. The solution will likely be slightly different based upon your investment objectives and where you're in the investment learning curve.

If you are just beginning, you might prioritize features like fundamental educational tools, comprehensive glossaries, simple access to support employees, and the capacity to put practice transactions before you begin playing with real cash.

In case you have any investment experience already under your belt, then but you are seeking to get serious, you might want more high-level instruction and opinion-based resources written by professional analysts and investors, in addition to a fantastic choice of technical and fundamental information.

A really seasoned investor, possibly someone who has implemented countless transactions but is searching for a new broker, will prioritize complex charting abilities, conditional order choices and the capability to exchange derivatives, mutual funds, commodities, and fixed-income securities, in addition to stocks.

Be honest with yourself about where you're right now in your own investing travel and in which you would like to go. Are you wishing to set a retirement fund and concentrate on passive income investments which can generate tax-free income within an IRA or even 401(k)? Would you need to try your hands in day-trading but do not know where to begin? Would you enjoy the concept of tweaking and tweaking your portfolio, or are you ready to pay an expert to ensure it is done correctly?

Based on which course you wish to follow, There Might Be many more Questions that you will want to answer along the way as you get expertise and develop your objectives. For the time being, however, begin with those four key considerations that will assist you figure out which of the broker features we discuss below would be important to you personally. To help capture those analytical juices flowing, we have included several sample queries below every wider subject:

- Generally speaking, are you an active or passive investor? Would you wish to be super hands free and implement afternoon - or swing-transactions? Can you see yourself finally leaving the 9-to-5 mill and getting a fulltime buyer? Or, rather, do you wish to get some strong investments to endure for the long haul with very little if any day-to-day interaction?

- Just how much do you know? What type of trades are you going to wish to do? Are you really going to be the kind of investor who is aware of what they wish to do and only wants a platform which makes it simple and fast to execute transactions, or do you desire a broker using a wider selection of tools that will assist you identify opportunities? What type of securities are you focused on? Stocks, mutual capital, ETFs? If you're more advanced, would you want to exchange options, futures, and fixed-income securities? How about margin trading? Do you require access to automatic orders, extended-hours trading, and automatic trading choices?

- Would you need assist? What type? Would you wish to go into the DIY path, find out how to interpret graphs and fiscal information to discover and execute your personal transactions, or in case you want to hire a professional? If you would like to do it yourself, where are you really on the learning curve? What type of resources are you going to have to enhance your own knowledge? Are you going to require simple access to support employees, or are you able to find out exactly what you want to understand through online educational tools? Are you really happy to perform trades online, or are you going to wish to phone in to get a broker help you with the procedure?

- Which are your objectives? What are you buying? Why are you choosing to spend? Have you been looking to enhance your regular income to improve your current standard of living? Is there a particular occasion or cost that you wish to finance? Do you need for it to finally become your principal revenue source? Are you currently attempting to develop retirement savings and, if yes, would you have a retirement accounts or are you going to wish to start out a new one along with your preferred broker?

There aren't any wrong answers to those queries. Be truthful with yourself roughly how much time, energy and effort you are willing and ready to place into your investments. Your answers can vary over time, and that is ok. Do not attempt to anticipate all of your requirements and aims for the remainder of your life. Just begin with where you are at this time.

Step 2: Narrow the Field
Now You Have a clear idea of exactly what your own investment goals are and What fundamental services that you'll search for in your perfect broker, it is time to whittle down

your choices somewhat. When there are definite brokerage characteristics that will be important for many traders than others, there are a couple things any respectable online broker should possess. With such a broad selection of available possibilities, assessing on those fundamental necessities is a fantastic way to narrow down the area fast.

Stock Broker Legislation and Trust

Is the broker a member of the Securities Investor Protection Corporation (SIPC)? There'll typically be some type of notation or disclaimer in the bottom of your home page. You are able to quickly find the broker on the SIPC site.

Is the broker a member of the Financial Industry Regulatory Authority (FINRA)? This ought to also be quite clearly noticed in an easy-to-find site. It is possible to look up brokerages on FINRA's BrokerCheck site.

When the broker Offers savings or checking account, or any additional deposit products, are they insured by the Federal Deposit Insurance Corporation (FDIC)? Investment commodities -- such as broker or retirement account that invest in stocks, bonds, choices, and annuities -- aren't FDIC guaranteed, since the value of investments can't be guaranteed. In case the broker offers CDs, Money Market Deposit Accounts (MMDAs), checking account, or savings account, nevertheless, they ought to be fully endorsed by the FDIC.

What Type of insurance do they Supply to guard you in the event the business fails? For a member of the SIPC, the business must have insurance using a per-customer limitation of $500,000, with $250,000 accessible for money promises. In the event the business adheres to the Client Protection Rule, then it also needs to give extra protection over and beyond the basic necessities of this SIPC.

Can there be any Sort of Guarantee of security from fraud? Can the company pay you for losses caused by fraud? Ensure that you double check exactly what the broker requires of you in order that you become reimbursed. Figure out in the event that you need to supply any documentation or require certain precautions to safeguard yourself.

Which are current Clients Expression? Try looking on the internet for customer reviews of this broker, using key words like "insurance claim, "fraud coverage" and "customer support." Needless to say, online testimonials should generally be taken with a grain of salt -- a few folks like to whine. But if there are many users from various websites all accommodation exactly the identical complaint then you might choose to explore further.

Online Security and Account Protection

It is important to know how well a broker can help you protect your information.

Does the broker Site Provide two-factor authentication? Can you have the choice of activating a safety attribute along with your password? Frequent options may include answering safety concerns, getting special, time-sensitive codes via text or email, or employing a physical security secret that matches into your USB port.

What Type of technology does the agent use to maintain your accounts safe? Find out whether the agent employs encryption or "cookies," and when it clearly describes how it uses them to secure your account info and the way in which they work.

Does the firm ever market Customer advice to third-parties, for example advertisers? The response should definitely be no.

Brokerage Account Offerings

Since the Kinds of tools you require will depend on your own Objectives, you should also do a fast check for these things to weed out brokerages that just will not fulfill your requirements.

What Types of accounts does the Broker offer besides conventional (nonrefundable) investment balances? By way of instance, if you have dependents, learn when you are able to start an Education Savings Account (ESA) or a custodial account for the child or other dependents.

Can you start a retirement account? Look into if the agent offers Roth or traditional retirement account and in the event that it is possible to roll over a present 401K or IRA.

Are there distinct goods for distinct investing objectives? By way of instance, find out whether the agent offers managed accounts. Additionally, figure out if there investment minimums for various kinds of accounts.

Can you handle retirement Accounts for workers throughout the brokerage? This can apply if you are a small business owner. These kinds of accounts comprise SIMPLE or SEP IRAs.

Does the broker offer Self-Directed IRAs or Solo 401K Choices? This applies if the sole employee on your business is that.

Step 3: Figure out the Charges

While there may be other things that matter more to you than charges, you should begin with a fairly clear idea of just how much you will pay to utilize any specific broker.

For many, a little premium could be justifiable if the stage provides Attributes that its cheaper competitors lack. Generally, however, you wish to lose as small of your investment yields as possible to bookkeeping fees and trading commissions.

By beginning with the bottom line, you can easily decide which inventory Agents are too expensive to think about and which simply are not compatible with the kind of investment action you are focused on.

Broker Account Fees

Does the broker charge a commission for launching an account?

Can there be a deposit minimal? Bear In mind that mutual funds frequently have investment minimums of $1,000 or more, but that is not exactly the same as a broker requiring that you deposit a minimum quantity of money simply to start an account.

Are there any yearly or monthly Account maintenance charges? If yes, are they waived for bigger accounts or is there a simple way to prevent them if your account balance is modest? By way of instance, Vanguard waives its yearly fee if account holders consent to receive records electronically.

Does the agent provide access to a trading platform as part of the free membership? If you are just beginning, the free platform will fit your requirements perfectly.

Can there be a Guru or Advanced Trading platform that's pay-to-play? If you are a more sophisticated investor, it is important that you learn whether you'll want to pay to upgrade your account to get resources and tools which are up for your pace. Some innovative platforms are free for clients who agree to put a minimal number of transactions each year or spend a minimal volume.

Which are the perimeter rates? Currency trading is only for experienced investors who know the dangers involved. If you are a new investor, this stage will not apply for you.

What is the minimum loan amount and account balance? Many brokerages will provide lower interest rates for larger numbers, but do not let this be why you borrow more than you need to.

Is your commission program conducive to the type of trading you would do? Have you been rewarded or penalized to get busier trading? By way of instance, Vanguard's commission prices rises after the initial 25 transactions for Standard and Flagship clients, or following the initial 100 transactions for Flagship Select clients, because you can see from the graph above. This means that clients that concentrate on passive, buy-and-hold investing reap the maximum benefit.

Additionally, E*TRADE provides reduced Commissions following the initial 30 transactions in any particular quarter, so busy dealers are rewarded for using the system more frequently.

When the agent provides advisory Providers, how much do they cost? Is there a minimum account balance required to be eligible for those services? If you are not seeking to control your portfolio for some reason, ensure that you look closely at adviser fees quite carefully.

Step 4: Examine the Broker's Platform

While any broker should have a fairly decent description of what sorts of resources and tools their trading platform provides, At times the best approach to estimate platform quality would be to give it a test drive. For agents that permit you to start an account at No Cost, it Might Even be worth the attempt to go through the signup procedure merely to get into the trading Platform if that is what is needed.

Whether the Broker has a Web-based platform that anybody can get or a free downloadable platform which needs no-strings signup, do everything you can to get into the tools you would really use at no cost.

Even if you're a more sophisticated Dealer, and there is no free way to have fun with "Guru" tools, you can find a fantastic idea of the caliber of a broker's offerings only by taking a look in its fundamental package. When there's nothing in the platform that appears promising, it is unlikely the advanced platform will probably be worth your time.

On the other hand, some businesses provide a massive variety of resources and tools using their free goods, and thus don't write off brokerages with no more than 1 platform only yet.

We have already spent a Fantastic amount of Time narrowing down your options based on cost and fundamental account offerings. Now that we have finally gotten into the fun things, ensure that you spend some time taking a look at the features offered in numerous places.

Proceed through the motions of setting a Trade to observe how easily the procedure operates. Pull up numerous estimates for shares and other securities, and then click on each tab to learn what sort of information the platform supplies. It's also wise to have a look at any accessible screeners or alternative tools supplied to assist you to find investments that satisfy particular criteria.

Questions to Answer While Testing Platforms

What Kinds of securities can you Trade on the stage? You should have mastered any platforms which don't permit you to exchange the securities you are considering. Ensure this platform automatically permit you to trade favorite stocks, IPOs, options, futures, or fixed-income securities. If you do not see specific security on the stage, but you are aware that the broker supports it, consider looking on your account preferences, or performing a fast search, to determine how you're able to activate those attributes and find out about consent requirements.

Are quotations in real time? Are they streaming? There'll be numerous methods you'll be able to pull a cost quote for any particular safety, however not all them will supply the most up-to-date information. Ensure that you know of where you are able to discover real-time streaming advice to make sure your transactions are well-timed. Vanguard's online platform, as an instance, supplies real-time information in its Ticker Profile webpages, but it needs manual sterile. Straightforward quote-level information is delayed by 20 minutes or longer. Schwab's online quotes additionally need manual sterile, but also the downloadable StreetSmart Edge platform and its own particular counterpart equally provide real time streaming information.

Can you install customized watchlists and alarms? If you are likely to become a more active dealer, you will probably wish to have the ability to get alert notifications through text, along with email, and install numerous watchlists based on various criteria.

Does the stage supply screeners you can personalize to locate stocks, ETFs, mutual funds, or other securities that satisfy your particular criteria? Even when you're brand-new and have no clue what some of these choices really mean, play with the many parameters to obtain a notion of just how simple the tools would be to use. A fantastic platform will be organized and simple to operate.

What Types of orders can you place? Proceed through the motions of setting a trade and have a peek at what kinds of orders are all offered. A fundamental platform should provide at least marketplace, limit, stop, and prevent limitation. An improved platform will also let you place tracking stop orders, or market-on-close orders (which implement in the cost the safety reaches market closure).

If you are looking to make comparatively few transactions, and you are not considering day- or swing-trading, a fundamental choice of order types must be OK. If you are trying to get in the nitty-gritty of stock trading, however, you should search for a broader choice. If you are more sophisticated, you should search for the capability to set conditional orders that enable you to install numerous transactions with particular triggers which can execute automatically when your specified requirements are satisfied.

Step 5: How Can the Stock Broker Educate Its Clientele?
Though a useful and usable trading platform Is Essential, you need to Also take some opportunity to peruse the broker's educational offerings and also test the search purpose.

If you are a new investor, You Have to Have the Ability to search for phrases you do not understand or find ideas for the best way best to interpret information. When there's a subject you have been wondering or a metric that you do not completely comprehend, do a trial run with the search function and see if you can locate the information that you need quickly and economically.

Bear in Mind, what is user-friendly and intuitive one buyer could be a Nightmarish listing of fruitless search questions for another, therefore it is essential to get a platform which it is possible to work with.

As Soon as you've spent 20 minutes or so cruising a stage, you need to be Able to answer these questions fairly readily. If you cannot, and a fast look of this website for particular answers does not yield the required information, it is probably a sign that the broker's platform isn't for you.

Stock Broker's Quality and Usability
Each of the instructional tools in the world are useless if you cannot Access them readily. A fantastic platform or site should offer a vast selection of educational offerings, in numerous mediums, to ensure clients can rapidly and easily discover the information that they require in a format that is right for their learning style. Before we dive into the particular kinds of

instructional tools you should expect out of a fantastic broker, let us first make sure that these tools are user-friendly.

Utilizing Paper Trading to Practice Day Trading

Day trading has become incredibly aggressive with the surge of high-speed trading and algorithmic trading happening from the markets. The fantastic thing is that a number of online agents have empowered newspaper trading accounts to aid traders hone their abilities before committing any true funds.

KEY TAKEAWAYS

- In case you are considering becoming a day trader, it is logical to find some sensible practice in first to check the waters.
- Paper trading is a means to mimic trading strategies and find out how they'd have paid, or maybe not, in fact.
- Online broker platforms progressively allow complex paper trading skills through demonstration accounts or as a characteristic for its present clients.

What's Paper Trading?

Paper trading is just another expression for trading, wherever People can purchase and sell securities without risking real money. As soon as it's likely to backtest trading approaches, traders could be tempted to use previous information to create present trades--called the look-ahead prejudice --although the incorrect backtesting dataset could entail a survivorship bias. Survivorship bias is the propensity to observe the operation of current funds in the marketplace as a representative sample.

Investors might have the ability to mimic trading using a simple spreadsheet or perhaps pen-and-paper, but day traders could have quite a challenging time recording hundreds or even thousands of transactions every day by hand and calculating their profits and losses. Fortunately, several internet agents and a few financial books provide paper trading account for people to practice with before committing actual funds to the marketplace. This lets them try out plans and practice working with the software.

Preparing a Day Trading Account
Day traders must ideally paper commerce with the identical day trading Agent they intend to utilize for their live accounts as it's going to be as near reality as you can.

As you look for the best location at which to practice your transactions, think about Paper trading platforms offering live marketplace feeds before you begin with actual funds. This is essential as you will want to have the ability to exchange without delayed processing or feeds orders.

One of the most well-known agents are Interactive Agents and TradeStation, which have fully-featured simulators that work with their automatic trading principles. Day traders employing these programs need to start an account to use the simulator, which might signify canceling the minimal funding requirements. The fantastic thing is that traders may use the simulator prior to making live trades using their own capital.

Online agents like Fidelity and TD Ameritrade also provide customers paper trade balances.

It is important to keep in mind that there are still some gaps between live and simulated trading. On a technical level, simulators might not account for slippage, commissions or spreads that may have a substantial effect on day trading yields. On a mental level, traders might have a simpler time sticking to trading platform rules without actual cash online -- especially when the trading process is not performing well.

Paper Trading Tips
Day trading clinic depends mostly on the plan that is used to exchange. As an instance, some day traders are concentrated on "sense" and have to rely upon paper trading account independently, but some utilize automated trading strategies and might backtest countless systems before newspaper trading just the most promising ones. Dealers should pick the

ideal broker platform to their needs according to their trading tastes and newspaper trade on these balances.

When newspaper trading, it is important to maintain an accurate listing of Trading performance and monitor the plan over a long time horizon. Some strategies might just operate in bull markets, so dealers could be captured off-guard every time a bear market comes together. It is important to check enough securities in many different market conditions so as to make sure their plans hold up efficiently and create the maximum risk-adjusted yields.

At length, paper trading is not a one-time-only job. Day traders should frequently utilize paper trading attributes in their broker accounts to check experimental and new approaches to test their hands into trading markets. Simple mistakes can be incredibly expensive for day traders that risk tens of thousands of dollars in tens of thousands of transactions every day. This makes newspaper trading an essential portion of long-term achievement.

Advantages of Paper Trading
Starting out with a paper trading accounts might help shorten your Learning curve. However there are different advantages beyond simply educating yourself. To begin with, you don't have any danger. As you are not using real cash, you do not

eliminate anything. It's possible to examine what errors you have created and help develop a winning plan. This also makes it possible to build your confidence, permits you to practice strategies and techniques required to become a successful day trader such as gain or reduction taking and pre-market preparation. Ultimately, it takes the strain from trading. It is possible to focus on your own plans in a comfortable environment and take the emotion out of gambling.

Disadvantages of Paper Trading
While paper trading can help give you the training you desire, there are a couple of downfalls. Since it does not use actual money, you do not have a notion of how commissions and fees variable into your own trades. All these simulators also don't accurately reflect the truth of these markets, together with the highs and lows along with the emotion that goes along with trading. Therefore, it's important to not forget this is a simulated environment as you get your trading abilities in check.

Practice, Practice, Practice
If you are a first-time investor, then take as much time as possible paper trading until you jump ship and start live trading. Make sure you explore unique approaches and fresh ideas so it's possible to get comfy. The theory behind using

simulators will be for you to find comfy and cut back on your learning curve.

When you feel like you have mastered everything you can Use a Simulator, try trading using a stock which has had a predictable run--using a lower cost and a constant response to market circumstances. If you begin trading with an extremely volatile inventory, it might be challenging. But should you decide on something safer, then you can practice what you've heard without taking on too much danger.

The Main Point

Day traders confront intense competition when it comes to successfully Identifying and executing commerce opportunities. Luckily, most online brokers provide paper trading performance that enables day traders to practice their skills before committing actual funds. Dealers should benefit from those features to protect against making expensive mistakes and optimize their long-term risk-adjusted yields and functionality.

CHAPTER FOUR

Risk & Money Management

A Guide to Day Trading on Margin

Day trading involves purchasing and selling exactly the very same stocks multiple occasions throughout trading hours in expectation of locking in rapid profits by the movement in stock rates. Day trading is insecure, as it is determined by the changes in stock prices on a single given day, and it may lead to substantial declines in a really brief time period.

KEY TAKEAWAYS
- Trading on margin permits you to borrow money from the broker so as to buy more stocks than the money on your accounts would permit for by itself. Currency trading also allows for short-selling.
- By utilizing leverage, margin enables you to amplify your prospective yields - along with your own losses.
- Margin calls and maintenance margin are needed, which may add up losses in case a transactions go sour.

Margin and Day Trading

Buying on margin, on the Other hand, is a tool which facilitates trading for people who don't possess the needed quantity of money available. Buying on margin enriches a dealer's buying power by letting them purchase for a larger amount when they have money for; the shortfall is stuffed by means of a brokerage company at interest. When the 2 tools are united in the kind of day trading margin, risks are highlighted. And moving from the dictum, "the greater the threat, the greater the possible return," The yields could be manifold. But be warned: there are not any warranties.

The Financial Industry Regulatory Authority (FINRA) rules specify a day commerce as "The buying and selling or the sale and buying of the identical security on exactly the exact same day in a margin account" The short-selling and buys to pay exactly the exact same security on precisely the exact same day together with choices also fall under the purview of a day commerce.

When we Discuss day trading, some may indulge inside only Sometimes and could have different margin requirements from individuals who could be labeled as "pattern day traders" Let us know these conditions together with the perimeter rules and prerequisites from FINRA.

A term routine day trader is employed for somebody who executes four or more day trades within five business days, given one of 2 points: 1) The amount of day transactions is greater than 6 percent of the total trades at the margin accounts during the exact same five-day period (or two) The individual indulges in 2 unmet day commerce calls in just a time span of 90 days. A non-pattern day dealer's account incurs day trading just sometimes.

But if some of the above mentioned criteria are satisfied, then a non-pattern day dealer accounts will be designated as a pattern day trader accounts. However, in case a pattern day trader's accounts hasn't completed daily transactions for 60 consecutive days, then its status is reversed into a non-pattern day dealer accounts.

Margin Requirements
To exchange on margin, investors should deposit enough money or qualified Securities that satisfy the first margin requirement using a broker company. According to the Fed's Legislation T, investors may borrow up to 50 percent of their entire price of buy on margin and the remaining 50 percent is deducted from the dealer as the initial margin requirement.

The maintenance margin demands to get a pattern day trader are far higher than that to get a non-pattern day dealer. The minimal equity demand to get a pattern day trader is $25,000 (roughly 25 percent of their entire market value of securities, whichever is greater) while for a non-pattern day dealer is

$2,000. Each day trading accounts must satisfy this condition individually rather than via cross-guaranteeing distinct accounts. In scenarios once the account falls under this specified amount of 25,000, additional trading isn't allowed until the account is replenished.

Margin Calls

A margin call happens if your account falls below the maintenance margin level. A margin call is a need from the broker for one to add cash to your accounts or shut out places to bring your account back to the necessary amount. If you don't meet the margin call, your brokerage company can close out any open places so as to bring the account up to the minimal price. Your brokerage company can do this with no approval and can select which place (s) to liquidate. Additionally, your broker company can bill you a commission for your trade (s). You're liable for any losses sustained in this procedure, along with your brokerage firm may manage enough contracts or shares to transcend the initial margin requirement.

Margin Buying Power

The purchasing power to get a Pattern day trader is four times that the surplus of the maintenance Margin at the closing of business of the preceding day (state an account Has $35,000 following the last day's transaction, then the surplus here is

10,000 as This sum is over and above the minimum requirement of $25,000. This would Provide a purchasing power of $40,000 (4 x $10,000). If this is exceeded, then the dealer will be given a day trading margin call issued from the brokerage company. There's a time period of five business days to satisfy up with the margin call. During this Interval, the day trading buying power is limited to 2 times the maintenance Margin surplus. In case of failure to satisfy the margin throughout the specified time Interval, additional trading is only permitted to get a cash available basis for 90 days, Or until the call has been fulfilled.

Instance of Trading Margin

Assume that a dealer has $20,000 over the maintenance margin amount. This will offer the trader using a day trading buying power of $80,000 (4 x $20,000). If the dealer succeeds in purchasing $80,000 of PQR Corp in 9:45 a.m. followed by $60,000 of XYZ Corp. in 10.05 a.m. on precisely the exact same day, then he's surpassed his purchasing power limitation. Even if he sells both throughout the day trade, he'll get a day trading margin call the following day. On the other hand, the dealer might have averted the margin call by selling off PQR Corp before purchasing XYZ Corp.

Notice: Even though the agents must operate within the parameters issued from the regulatory authorities, they have the discretion to make minor alterations from the set requirements known as "home requirements." A broker-dealer can classify a client for a pattern day trader by bringing them under their wider definition of a pattern day trader. Additionally, brokerage companies may impose increased margin requirements or confine buying electricity. Therefore, there may be variations depending on the broker-dealer you opt to trade with.

The Main Point

Day trading on margin is a risky exercise and Shouldn't Be attempted by novices. Individuals who have expertise daily trading also will need to take care when using margin to exactly the same. Employing margin provides traders an improved buying power nonetheless; it needs to be used wisely daily trading so that dealers don't wind up incurring substantial losses. Allowing yourself to constraints set to your margin accounts can lessen the margin requirements and thus the requirement for extra funds. If you're looking for day trading for the first time, do not experiment using a margin accounts.

Economy Risk

Market risk is the possibility of an Investor undergoing losses because of factors which impact the general functioning of the monetary markets where he or she's involved. Economy risk, also known as "systematic threat," can't be eliminated through diversification, even though it could be hedged against in different ways. Resources of market risk comprise recessions, political chaos, and changes in rates of interest, natural disasters and terrorist attacks. Systematic, or market risk will affect the whole market at precisely the exact same moment.

This may be contrasted with unsystematic risk, which can be unique to a particular business or industry. Also called "nonsystematic risk, "particular risk, "diversifiable risk" or "residual danger," in the context of an investment portfolio, unsystematic risk can be decreased via diversification.

KEY TAKEAWAYS
- Economy threat, or systematic risk, impacts the functioning of the full market concurrently.
- Since it impacts the entire market, it isn't easy to hedge as diversification won't help.
- Market threat could entail adjustments to interest rates, exchange rates, geopolitical events, or recessions.

Understanding Market Risk

Economy (systematic) risk and particular risk (unsystematic) make up both main kinds of investment risk. The most typical forms of market risks include interest rate risk, equity risk, currency risk and commodity risk.

Publicly traded firms in America are needed by the Securities and Exchange Commission (SEC) to disclose their results and productivity could possibly be connected to the operation of the financial markets. This condition is supposed to detail an organization's vulnerability to financial risk. By way of instance, a firm supplying derivative investments or foreign exchange futures may be exposed to financial risk than firms which don't offer these kinds of investments. This information helps traders and investors make conclusions based on their particular risk management principles.

Compared to promote risk, certain risk or "unsystematic risk" is tied directly to the functionality of a specific safety and may be guarded against investment diversification. 1 instance of unsystematic risk is that a company declaring bankruptcy, thus making its inventory useless to investors.

Main Types of Market Risk

Interest rate risk covers the volatility which may accompany interest rate changes as a result of fundamental aspects, such as central bank statements linked to fluctuations in financial policy. This risk is the most important to investments in fixed-income securities, like bonds.

Equity risk is the danger involved with the shifting prices of inventory Assets, and commodity threat covers the changing prices of commodities like crude oil and corn.

Money risk, or Exchange-rate risk, originates from the shift in the purchase price of one currency in relation to another; investors or companies holding assets in a different country are susceptible to currency risk.

Volatility and Hedging Market Risk

Market risk is different due to cost fluctuations. The standard deviation of Fluctuations in the prices of shares, commodities or currencies is called price volatility. Volatility is ranked in annualized terms and could be expressed as an absolute amount, for example $10, or some proportion of the first price, for example 10%.

Investors may use hedging approaches to protect against volatility and market risk. Targeting certain investors, investors can purchase set options to shield against a disadvantage movement, and investors that wish to hedge a huge portfolio of shares may use index choices.

Measuring Market Risk

To quantify market risk, analysts and investors utilize the value-at-risk (VaR) method. VaR modeling is a statistical risk management system which quantifies a stock or portfolio possible loss in addition to the likelihood of the possible loss happening. While well-known and broadly used, the VaR method requires particular assumptions that restrict its precision. As an instance, it presumes that the content and makeup of the portfolio has been quantified is unchanged within a predetermined period. Though this might be suitable for short term horizons, it might provide less precise measurements for long-term investments.

Beta is just another related hazard metric, as it measures the volatility or market risk of a portfolio or security compared with the market as a whole; it's employed from the capital asset pricing model (CAPM) to compute the expected return of an asset.

Risk Control Strategies for Active Traders

Risk Management helps reduce losses. In addition, it can help safeguard a dealer's accounts from losing all his or her cash. The danger takes place when the trader suffers a reduction. If it could be handled it, the dealer can open himself or herself up to earning money on the marketplace.

It's an essential but often overlooked requirement to successful active trading. In the end, a dealer who has generated considerable profits can lose everything in only a couple of bad trades with no proper risk management plan. So how can you build the best techniques to suppress the dangers of the marketplace?

This guide will talk about some basic strategies which may be utilized to safeguard your trading gains.

KEY TAKEAWAYS
- Trading could be exciting and even rewarding if you're able to remain focused, do due diligence, and keep emotions at bay.
- However, the very best dealers will need to integrate risk management methods to prevent losses from becoming out of hands.
- Using a tactical and objective method of cutting losses through stop orders, profit taking, and protective puts is a wise way to keep in the game.

Planning Your Trades
As Chinese army General Sun Tzu's famously stated: "Each Battle is won before it's fought." This term implies that strategy and planning --not the conflicts --win wars. In the same way,

successful traders typically estimate the term: "Plan the commerce and trade the strategy." Exactly like in warfare, moving ahead can often mean the difference between failure and success.

First, ensure that your agent is ideal for regular trading. Some Agents cater to clients who trade infrequently. They charge high commissions and do not supply the ideal analytical tools for active traders.

Stop-loss (S/L) and take-profit (T/P) points signify two important ways that traders may plan ahead when trading. Successful traders know what cost they're prepared to cover and at what cost they're ready to sell. They could then quantify the resulting returns from the likelihood of the inventory hitting their targets. If the adjusted yield is large enough, they implement the transaction.

Conversely, ineffective dealers frequently enter a trade with no idea of the points where they'll sell at a gain or a loss. Like gamblers onto a lucky--or unlucky streak--feelings start to take over and order their transactions. Losses frequently induce individuals to continue and expect to earn their money back, while gains can lure traders to imprudently continue for much more profits.

Contemplate the One-Percent Rule

A good deal of day dealers follow what is known as the one-percent rule. Essentially, this rule of thumb indicates that you shouldn't place more than one% of your funds or your own trading accounts into one trade. Therefore, in the event that you have $10,000 on your trading accounts, your position in any particular instrument should not be greater than $100.

This strategy is Typical for traders that have balances of less than $100,000--a few even go as large as 2 percent if they could afford it. Many dealers whose accounts have greater balances might opt to choose a lesser percent. That is because as the dimensions of your accounts increases, so also does the position. The very best way to maintain your losses is to maintain the rule under 2 percent --some more and you would be risking a considerable sum of your trading accounts.

Placing Stop-Loss and Take-Profit Points

A stop-loss stage is that the cost at which a dealer will sell a stock and Have a loss on the transaction. This frequently occurs when a transaction doesn't pan out how a dealer expected. The points are made to protect against the "it'll return" mindset and restrict losses before they escalate. By way of instance, if a stock breaks below an integral support level, traders frequently sell whenever possible.

On the other hand, a take-profit stage is the cost at which a dealer will sell a stock and have a profit on the transaction. This can be when the extra upside is restricted given the dangers. By way of instance, if a stock is approaching a crucial resistance level following a sizable move up, traders might want to market in front of a period of consolidation occurs.

How to Efficiently Set Stop-Loss Points
Placing stop-loss and take-profit points can be done using specialized Analysis, but basic analysis may play an integral role in time. By way of instance, if a dealer is holding a stock before earnings because excitement builds, they might want to sell before the news hits the marketplace if expectations are now too high, whether or not the take-profit cost was hit.

Moving averages represent the very popular way to place these things, as they're not hard to compute and broadly monitored by the marketplace. Crucial moving averages include the 5-, 9-, 20-, 50-, and 100- and - 200-day averages. All these are best set using them to some stock's graph and ascertaining if the stock price has responded to them previously as a support or resistance level.

Another Fantastic Way to put stop-loss or take-profit amounts is to Resistance or support trend lines. These could be brought on by linking previous highs or lows that happened on important, above-average quantity. Like moving averages, the important thing is determining levels where the cost responds to the fashion lines and, clearly, on large volume.

When placing those things, here are some key factors:

- Use longer-term moving averages to get much more volatile stocks to decrease the possibility that a futile price swing will activate a stop-loss sequence to be implemented.
- Fix the moving averages to accommodate target cost ranges. By way of instance, longer goals should use bigger moving averages to decrease the amount of signs generated.
- Cease losses shouldn't be nearer than 1.5-times the present high-to-low scope (volatility), since it's too likely to get implemented without reason.
- Fix the stop loss in line with the market's volatility. If the stock price is not moving too much, then the stop-loss points could be tightened.
- Utilize known basic incidents such as earnings releases, as crucial time intervals to maintain or from a commerce as uncertainty and volatility can grow.

Calculating Expected Yield

Placing stop-loss and take-profit points will also be necessary to Figure out the anticipated return. The significance of this calculation can't be overstated, since it forces traders to consider their transactions and rationalize them. At the same time, it provides them a systematic method to compare several trades and choose only the most lucrative ones.

This can be calculated with the following formula:

[(Probability of Profit) x (Require Gain% Profit)] + [(Probability of reduction) x (Stop-Loss% reduction)]

The result of this calculation is the expected return for the busy Dealer that will subsequently measure it against other chances to ascertain which stocks to trade. The likelihood of profit or loss may be computed by employing historic breakouts and breakdowns in the support or resistance levels--or for seasoned dealers, by creating an educated guess.

Diversify and Hedge

Ensuring you Take Advantage of your trading means not placing your Eggs in 1 basket. If you set all of your money in 1 stock or a single tool, you are setting yourself up for a large reduction. So be sure to diversify your investments--around the market sector in addition to market capitalization and geographical region. Does this assist you to manage your danger, but in addition, it opens you up to greater chances.

You may also find a time when you want to hedge your own position. Think about a stock position once the outcomes are expected. You might think about taking the contrary position through choices, which may help safeguard your position. When trading action subsides, you may then unwind the Dollar.

Downside Set Choices

If you're approved for options trading, purchasing a downside place Alternative, sometimes called a protective place, may also be utilized as a hedge to stem losses from a transaction that turns sour. A put option provides you the best, but not the obligation, to sell the underlying stock at a given priced at or before the option expires. Thus in the event that you have XYZ inventory from $100 and purchase the 6-month $80 place for $1.00 per choice in superior, then you'll be effectively stopped from any cost fall below $79 ($80 strike minus the $1 premium paid).

The Main Point

Dealers should know when they intend to enter or exit a transaction before they implement. Using stop losses efficiently, a dealer can diminish not just losses but also the amount of times every transaction is left needlessly. In summary, make your battle strategy beforehand so that you'll already know you have won the war.

Risk/Reward Ratio Definition

The risk/reward ratio marks the Potential reward an investor could make, for each and every dollar he or she risks in an investment. Many investors use risk/reward ratios to compare the anticipated returns of an investment together with the total amount of danger they need to undertake to make these returns. Consider the following instance: an investment using a risk-reward ratio of 1:7 indicates that an investor is prepared to gamble $1, to get the possibility of earning 7. Alternately, a risk/reward ratio of 1:3 indicates an investor must expect to spend $1, for the possibility of earning 3 on his investment.

Dealers often use this strategy to strategy which transactions to take, and also the ratio is calculated by dividing the sum a dealer stands to lose if the purchase price of an asset goes in an unexpected direction (the danger) from the total amount of gain the dealer expects to get made while the place is closed (that the reward).

KEY TAKEAWAYS
- The risk/reward ratio is used by dealers to handle their funds and risk of loss during gambling.
- The ratio helps evaluate the expected return and risk of a certain trade.
- A fantastic risk reward ratio will be anything higher than 1.

The way the Risk/Reward Ratio Works

The risk/reward ratio is often used as a step when trading individual stocks. The best risk/reward ratio differs widely amongst different trading strategies. Some trial-and-error approaches are often required to ascertain which ratio is ideal for a given trading plan, and lots of investors have a pre-specified risk/reward ratio to their trades.

Oftentimes, market strategists locate the perfect risk/reward ratio due to their own investments to be roughly 1:3, or 3 components of anticipated return for each 1 unit of further risk. Investors may handle risk/reward more straight through the usage of stop-loss derivatives and orders like set options.

Risk/Reward Ratio

What Can the Risk/Reward Ratio Inform You?

The risk/reward ratio assists investors manage their danger of shedding Cash on transactions. Even if a dealer has some lucrative trades, he'll eliminate money over time when his triumph rate is under 50%. The risk/reward ratio measures the gap between a transaction entry points to some stop-loss along with a market or take-profit purchase. Comparing these two supplies the proportion of gain to loss, or benefit to danger.

Investors frequently use stop-loss orders when trading stocks to help decrease losses and immediately manage their investments using a risk/reward focus. A stop-loss purchase is a trading cause put on a stock which overlooks the sale of the inventory from a portfolio when the stock reaches a predetermined low. Investors may automatically place stop-loss orders via brokerage accounts and generally do not need exorbitant extra trading expenses.

Instance of this Risk/Reward Ratio in Use
Consider this case: A dealer buys 100 shares of XYZ Company in $20 and puts a stop-loss purchase at $15 to make sure that losses won't exceed $500. Additionally, assume that this dealer thinks that the purchase price of XYZ will likely reach $30 in the upcoming few months. In cases like this, the dealer is prepared to gamble $5 per share to produce an estimated yield of $10 per share after closing the position. Considering that the dealer stands to create double the quantity which she's risked, she'd be said to have a 1:2

risk/reward ratio on that specific trade. Derivatives contracts like place contracts, which provide their owners the right to sell the underlying asset at a predetermined cost, may be used to similar effect.

If a conservative investor expects a 1:5 risk/reward ratio to get a Predetermined investment (five components of expected return for every extra unit of Risk), then he may use the stop-loss sequence to correct the risk/reward ratio to His very own specification. In Cases like This, from the trading case noted above, in case an Investor has a 1:5 risk/reward ratio needed because of his investment, he'd place the stop-loss purchase at $18 instead of $15--which is, he's more risk-averse.

CHAPTER FIVE

Day Trading Psychology

Trading psychology refers to the Emotions and psychological state which help dictate success or failure in trading securities. Trading psychology reflects various aspects of an individual's character and behaviors that influence their trading activities. Trading psychology can be as essential as other features such as knowledge, experience and skill in determining trading success.

Discipline and risk-taking are just two of the most critical facets of trading psychology, since a dealer's implementation of those aspects is vital to the achievement of her or his trading plan. While fear and greed are the two most commonly known emotions associated with trading psychology, and other emotions which induce trading behavior are hope and sorrow.

KEY TAKEAWAYS
- Trading psychology is the psychological component of investor's decision making process which may help explain why some decisions seem more logical than others.

- Trading psychology is characterized primarily because the effect of both greed and fear.
- Greed drives decisions that seem to accept too much risk.
- Fear drives decisions that seem to prevent danger and generate too little return.

Recognizing Trading Psychology

Trading psychology can be associated with a few unique emotions and Behaviors which are often catalysts for market trading. Traditional characterizations of emotionally-driven behavior in markets ascribe most psychological trading to greed or fear.

Greed is thought of as an excessive desire for wealth, so excessive it clouds rationality and conclusion sometimes. Thus this characterization of greed-inspired investor or trading presumes that this emotion often leads traders towards a variety of behaviors. This may include making trades that are risky, purchasing shares of an untested company or technology simply because it is going up in price quickly, or buying stocks without exploring the underlying investment.

Additionally, greed may inspire investors to Remain in profitable trades more than is advisable in a bid to squeeze out extra gains from it, or even to take on large speculative positions. Greed is most apparent in the final period of bull markets, when speculation runs rampant and investors throw caution to the end.

Conversely, anxiety causes traders to shut positions or to refrain from taking on danger because of concern about big losses. Fear is real during bear markets, and it's a potent emotion which can result in traders and investors to behave irrationally in their haste to exit the market. Fear often morphs to panic, which normally induces substantial selloffs on the marketplace from fear selling.

Regret may cause a trader to get into a trade after originally missing Out on it since the stock proceeded too fast. This is a violation of trading discipline and often results in direct losses from security costs that are falling from peak highs.

Technical Analysis

Trading psychology is frequently important for specialized analysts emphasizing on charting techniques to drive their commerce decisions. Security charting can offer a wide array of insights on a safety's movement. While technical evaluation and charting methods can be helpful in discovering trends for buying and selling opportunities, it requires an understanding and intuition for market movements that's derived from an investor's trading psychology.

There are numerous instances in specialized charting where a trader needs to Rely not just on the chart's insight but also their particular knowledge of the safety they're following and their instinct for how wider factors are impacting the market. Traders with a keen focus to comprehensive security cost affects, discipline and confidence reveal a balanced trading psychology that generally leads to profitable success.

The Importance of Trading Psychology

Many skills are needed for trading successfully in the financial markets. They include the skills to evaluate a company's fundamentals and to ascertain the direction of a stock's trend. But neither of those technical skills is as important as the trader's mindset.

Containing emotion, thinking fast, and exercising area are elements of what we might call trading psychology.

There are two chief emotions to understand and maintain under control: fear and greed.

Snap Decisions

Traders frequently have to believe fast and make fast choices, darting in and from shares on short notice. To accomplish this, they need a certain presence of mind. They also want the discipline to stay with their particular trading plans and understand when to book gains and losses. Emotions simply can't get in the way.

KEY TAKEAWAYS

- Overall investor sentiment frequently drives market functionality in directions that are at odds with the fundamentals.
- The effective investor controls fear and greed, the two human emotions that drive that sentiment.
- Recognizing this can provide you the discipline and objectivity required to take advantage of others' emotions.

Knowing Stress

When dealers receive bad news for a certain stock or on the market In general, they naturally get scared. They could overreact and feel pressured to liquidate their holdings and sit on the cash, refraining from taking any more risks. If they do, they may avoid specific losses but may also overlook some profits.

Dealers will need to understand what fear is: a natural response to a perceived threat. In cases like this, it's a danger to their profit possible.

Quantifying the anxiety might help. Traders should consider just what they are afraid of, and why they are fearful of it. But that thinking should occur before the bad news, not in the middle of it.

Stress and Greed are the two visceral emotions to keep in control.

By believing it through ahead of time, traders will know how they Perceive events intuitively and respond to them, and also may proceed past the emotional response. Obviously, this isn't easy, but it's vital to the wellbeing of an investor's portfolio, and of course the investor.

Overcoming Greed

There is an old saying on Wall Street that "pigs get slaughtered." This pertains to the habit greedy investors have of clinging on to a winning place too long to have every last tick upward in price. Sooner or later, the trend reverses and the greedy get caught.

Greed isn't easy to conquer. It is often based on the instinct to do better, for just a bit more. A trader must learn to comprehend this instinct and create a trading strategy based on rational thinking, not whims or instincts.

Placing Rules

A dealer needs to produce principles and follow along when the Psychological crunch comes. Establish guidelines based on your own risk-reward tolerance for if to enter a transaction and when to exit it. Set a profit target and put a stop reduction in place to take emotion out of this procedure.

In addition, you might decide which specific events, such as a Negative or positive earnings release, should trigger a decision to purchase or sell a stock.

It is Sensible to set limits on the maximum amount you're willing to win or lose daily. Should you reach the profit target, take the cash and run. If your losses reach a predetermined amount, fold your tent and go home.

Either way, you are going to live to trade another day.

Conducting Research and Review

Traders will need to become specialists in the stocks and industries that interest them. Keep on top of the information, instruct yourself and, if possible, visit trading conventions and attend conventions.

Devote as much time as possible to the study procedure. That means Studying charts, speaking with direction, reading trade journals, and doing other background work like macroeconomic analysis or industry analysis.

Knowledge can also help overcome anxiety.

Stay Flexible

It's important for dealers to Stay flexible and consider experimenting from time to time. By way of instance, you might consider using alternatives to mitigate risk. One of the best ways a trader can find out is by experimenting (within reason). The encounter may also help lessen emotional influences.

Finally, traders must periodically evaluate their own performances. In Addition to assessing their returns and respective places, traders should reflect on how they ready for a trading session, how up to date they are about the markets, and also how they're progressing in terms of ongoing education. This periodic evaluation can help a trader correct mistakes, change bad habits, and also enhance overall yields.

5 Day Trading Strategies for Beginners

Day trading is the action of purchasing and selling a financial tool within precisely the same day or even multiple occasions over the course of a day. Taking advantage of small price moves can be a lucrative match --if it is played properly. However, it can be a dangerous game for novices or anyone who doesn't stick to a well-thought-out strategy.

Not all brokers are satisfied to the high volume of trades made by day dealers, however. But some brokers are designed with all the day trader in your mind. You may check out our list of this best brokers for day trading to see which agents best accommodate individuals who would like to day trade.

Online brokers on our list, such as Tradestation, TD Ameritrade, and Interactive Agents, have professional or advanced versions of the platforms which feature real-time streaming quotes, advanced charting tools, and also the capacity to enter and modify complex orders in fast succession.

Below, we'll take a look at some overall day trading principles and then proceed to deciding when to buy and sell, common day trading approaches, basic charts and patterns, and how to limit losses.

KEY TAKEAWAYS
- Day trading is only rewarding when traders take it seriously and do their research.
- Day trading is a job, not a hobby; treat it as such--be diligent, focused, goal, and keep emotions out of it.

Here we offer some basic tips and know-how to become a successful day trader.

Day Trading Strategies

1. Knowledge Is Power
Besides knowledge of basic trading procedures, traders need to keep up on the latest stock market news and events that influence stocks--the Fed's interest plans, the economic outlook, etc.

So do your assignments. Create a wish list of shares you'd love to exchange and keep yourself informed about the selected companies and overall markets. Scan company news and see reliable financial websites.

2. Set Aside Funds
Evaluate how much capital you are prepared to risk on every trade. Many Successful day traders risk less than 1% to 2 percent of their account per trade. If you've got a $40,000

trading account and will willingly risk 0.5percent of your capital on each trade, your maximum loss per trade is $200 (0.5% $40,000).

Set aside too much of money you can exchange with and you're prepared to lose. Remember, it may or may not happen.

3. Set Aside Time, Too

Day trading requires your own time. That is why it's called trading. You will want to give up most of your day, actually. Don't think about it if you have little time to spare.

The Method requires a trader to track the markets and place Opportunities, which may arise at any time during trading hours. Moving fast is key.

4. Start Small

As a beginner, focus on a maximum of one to two stocks throughout a session. Tracking and locating opportunities is easier with just a few stocks. Lately, it has become more and more common to have the ability to exchange fractional shares, so you can define particular, smaller dollar numbers you would like to make investments.

That implies if Apple stocks are trading at $250 and you only want to buy $50 value, many agents will now let you buy one-fifth of a talk.

5. Prevent Penny Stocks

You're probably looking for bargains and low prices but stay away from penny stocks. These stocks are usually illiquid, and chances of hitting a jackpot are usually bleak.

Many stocks trading under $5 a share turned into de-listed from important stock Exchanges and are only tradable over-the-counter (OTC). Unless you see a real chance and have completed your research, remain clear of these.

www.ingramcontent.com/pod-product-compliance
Lightning Source LLC
Chambersburg PA
CBHW071127240526
45465CB00024B/1475